CHATTER BOX:
My Life with Autism,
A Mother and Sons Perspective

CHATTER BOX:
My Life with Autism,
A Mother and Sons Perspective

Martin Slyngstad & Stella Slyngstad

ARCHWAY
PUBLISHING

Archway Publishing books may be ordered through booksellers or by contacting:

Archway Publishing
1663 Liberty Drive
Bloomington, IN 47403
www.archwaypublishing.com
844-669-3957

ISBN: 978-1-6657-4655-7 (sc)
ISBN: 978-1-6657-4656-4 (e)

Library of Congress Control Number: 2023912109

Print information available on the last page.

Archway Publishing rev. date: 07/18/2023

MARTIN'S DEDICATION

To my grandma "Mae" (gone but never forgotten).

To my dad Todd. You showed me many terrific things and experiences. You made me want to explore. Love you Dad.

To my brother, Matthew. It wasn't easy being my brother. I know this and I love you.

To my extended family: stepmother, stepfather, stepbrothers, stepsisters, aunts, uncles, and cousins. We are a deeply close family and I appreciate all your support throughout my life.

Special thanks to Pete Pallares and Armando Luna-Medina for believing I could do this.

To Michelle Garcia Winner and Randy Dodge for teaching me to be social – a lifelong process.

To my church family. Thank you for all your prayers and encouragement.

I would never have written this book without my family's support. Having you all there supporting me through my struggles in life with autism has not gone unnoticed. You're the best and I appreciate you all. You all mean so much to me. I love you and thank you. I want to thank God most of all because without Him none of this is possible.

STELLA'S DEDICATION

To my son, Martin. Thank you for being funny, kind, challenging, understanding, not understanding, and honest.

I love everything about you.

CONTENTS

Martin's Dedication v

Stella's Dedication vii

Foreword xi

Martin's Preface... xiii

Mom's Preface xv

Chapter 1 1
    Martin: Early Years 1
    Mom: Early Years 2

Chapter 2 6
    Martin: Disabilities 6
    Mom: Disabilities 12

Chapter 3 14
    Martin: Anxiety 14
    Mom: Anxiety 17

Chapter 4 18
    Martin: Hobbies 18
    Mom: Hobbies 27

Chapter 5 28
    Martin: Friendships 28
    Mom: Friendships 31

Chapter 6 33
    Martin: School & Teachers 33
    Mom: School & Teachers 37

Chapter 7 40
    Martin: Spirituality 40
    Mom: Spirituality 41
Chapter 8 42
    Martin: Uber 42
    Mom: Uber 43
Chapter 9 45
    Martin: Dating 45
    Mom: Dating 47
Chapter 10 49
    Martin: Work 49
    Mom: Work 52

Martin's Final Thoughts 53
Mom's Final Thoughts 57
Resources 59
Acknowledgements 61

FOREWORD

Sometimes in life, we are lucky enough to meet someone that just leaves you a better person; Martin is one of those people. He has a not so quiet dedication to himself and a fearless forward motion despite his fears and limitations. Martin has always been a talker, a dreamer, and a doer. And he has probably done more things in his short life than most of us will ever get to do in a lifetime. This is not only due to his parents but to his constant desire to better himself. To go and do things on his own or by subtly or not so subtly, persuading some family member to do it with him. I am his aunt and his godmother. I was his go-to partner for fitness expos and MMA fights, his cousins were go-to partners for football, baseball, and soccer games. If there was something he wanted to do or some direction he felt he needed to go, he would call and at first hint around a subject followed by "when can I schedule that," or "I'll look into dates and get back to you," which he did. If he wasn't sure about something, he would say, "I'll get back to you on that." The funny thing is that in this process of Martin finding a companion to accompany him to an event, he kept this family together. God works in mysterious ways; the things He mysteriously creates are sometimes healers for everyone involved. We are blessed to have Martin as this beautiful, unique glue that binds our hearts together in the funniest of ways.

Sports: Martin loves sports. He can tell you anything about every sports game out there, players, stats, you name it, he has an answer for you. If he doesn't, he will find it and then never again forget it. It is indeed a gift; I have used that gift a few times. I've been at events where people are discussing certain sporting events or players that I know nothing about; a quick call to Martin, and I'm suddenly well versed.

I have seen this beautiful soul overcome so much from the rejection and ridicule of his peers, to the costly struggle with Asperger's, to the surgical procedure that left his entire back held together by titanium rods, the divorce of his parents, and integration into new extended families. Despite his fears, he continually attended school through successes and failures to find a career that truly excites him. One thing about Martin; if he knows what he wants, he will wholeheartedly fight to get it, like a steam engine without a braking system. How could you not admire that constant forward motion personality?

I am honored that Martin asked me to write this. My words cannot honestly explain the magnitude of what he brings to this family. He is our blessing, and a reminder not to quit but to find a better way.

A real example is if one thing doesn't work, then try something else, and if that doesn't work, try again and again and again. If no one wants to go, he goes alone; that's a hard thing to do, and yet he does it. I admire everything about him. He has made me a better version of myself.

I love him to pieces.
Rachel Rowberry

MARTIN'S PREFACE

Hello all, my name is Martin. I decided to write this book for a couple of reasons. First and foremost, I wanted to share my story about living on the autism spectrum. Writing this book has not been easy for me, and I feel vulnerable. At one point, I didn't write anything for two years because I was afraid people might not like my book. Anxiety hit me so hard, I wanted to give up and not tell my story. I am breaking out of my shell big time with this one, and I can't let this anxiety take control of me. The second reason I am writing this book is to help others with autism break through their shells, encourage them, and inform them that, as Bob Marley says, "every little thing will be all right". This book is also for people who don't know about autism, who don't have it, and who want to know more about it or understand it better. It is hard for me to watch other people on the spectrum struggle with everyday things. I hope that this book will empower others on the spectrum to get through the struggles that they face, and educate those around them on what it is like living with autism.

The *American Journal of Psychiatry* reports there is a large population of autistic people here in the United States, ranking just behind South Korea with a rate of one in thirty-eight people with autism. Given those statistics, I thought this would be the perfect time to tell my story. This book will make you laugh, shed a few tears (maybe), inspire (I hope), and encourage you to break out of your shell, live life to the fullest, and not let anxiety stop you from doing what you enjoy. I will admit, I still have anxiety talking about autism, but not as much as I did before I decided to write this, although it comes in random spurts. I put a lot of effort into making this since a lot of subjects were not easy to discuss, and I hope that this book will positively impact your life. I also hope this book will help encourage you to live your best life, and know you are capable.

MOM'S PREFACE

Martin was so excited when I suggested that we write a book about our experience. Once we started writing, it became a diary, and seven years later we are still at it. In the process of writing this book, Martin and I did not read each other's chapters until the entirety of the book had been completed. Writing about our experiences, looking back at how far we have come, wow! It has been healing, courageous, and scary. I've enjoyed every moment of writing this book.

If you are a parent of a child with Asperger's (affectionately known as an aspie) then you know why this book is titled Chatter Box. My niece, Melissa DaPonte, thought of the title, and it's very fitting considering our aspie kids love to talk and talk and talk about everything and then some.

You get two perspectives in this book: from an Asperger son and a mom raising him. Martin and I chose topics, and we both wrote about our thoughts and experiences. I must add, Martin didn't like the title, but agreed he does like to talk to this day. Martin especially wants to talk when I'm on the phone. Martin has a great sense of humor. One night he decided to have a stare down with a raccoon in the back yard. I asked him why he was doing this, and his response was, "I was trying to be the big man, but I wasn't." The raccoon won. I love our aspie kids. There is a naiveté about them and yet there can be so much knowledge. They love to share with you all the time. It can be simultaneously exhausting and enjoyable. I am eternally grateful to my family, moms, teachers, doctors, physical therapists, speech therapists, and occupational therapists that have taught and helped along the way. It takes a village! I especially give thanks to God for all his guidance and patience, and for leading me in a positive direction during this time of ups and downs.

I decided to write this book with Martin for two reasons: healing myself and telling my story about raising an aspie. It's okay to be discouraged and to question yourself, well, every day. I can't count how many times I was discouraged, but when you love someone this much, you keep it together and you keep going. As parents, we need to understand our children, and so our mission begins.

> The CDC estimates that about 1 in 44 children have been identified with ASD this year (2021). These estimates are from the ADDM (Autism and Developmental Disabilities Monitoring) Network.

"My life is like a road, not any one though. It is like an uncharted road with some roadblocks and blind turns, not knowing where the next turn will be taking me. But I know this: I am ready for wherever this road will lead and whatever roadblocks that I may face. And I want to say this: whatever roadblock you face, push forward."

- Martin Slyngstad

CHAPTER 1

Martin: Early Years

My story began when I was born. I was born in November at Good Samaritan Hospital in San Jose, California.

When I turned three, I was diagnosed with autism and Non-verbal Learning Disorder (NLD) at Stanford Research Center. Autism is a developmental disorder of varying severity that is characterized by difficulty in social interaction and communication and by repetitive patterns of thought and behavior. NLD is a learning disability that causes difficulty with motor, visual, spatial, and social skills. At one point they put me on some medications like Ritalin, but that never helped; it made me worse. When I was twelve, I was diagnosed with scoliosis, which caused my back to have a curve. Not only that, but they found a non-cancerous tumor. Which this caused my back to fracture from the top of my neck to the bottom of my back, which in doctor language means T3 (Thoracic) to L5 (Lumbar), so that was not good. I had spine surgery on August 1st, 2006. They put two rods and eighteen bolts in my back (the lower-left screw popped out). I was disappointed with my luck, and couldn't figure out why I had scoliosis, or why I was dealt a hand like this.

When I was four years old, I played soccer. It was and still is a fun sport to play, although I haven't played much in the past fourteen years because of my spine condition. Scoliosis limits things and you can't play the sports you most loved. If I were to fall, or get hit, or even twist, then the rods in my back could break, and I would have to go in for a second surgery, which would be terrible.

Our family lived on Mount Hamilton for about ten years, and it was fun. One year it snowed enough for my mother and me to ski down our road. Mt. Hamilton is the home of Lick Observatory, and one of my neighbors was an astronomer. He would let me check out the mini planetarium that he built in his back yard. In that planetarium, there was a telescope with a roof that opened so you could look at the stars. The telescope was so powerful I could amazingly see the stars and planets in broad daylight, which was unique.

Mom: Early Years

Every milestone was challenging: crawling, walking, talking, playing, coordination, and spatial awareness. Martin's developmental milestones were delayed. He couldn't sit without help until he was eighteen months old. He started walking independently at twenty-two months, after just learning to crawl a short time prior. He began to feed himself with his fingers at eighteen months of age and preferred to use his fingers for years. Feeding himself with utensils was a difficult task. He rode a tricycle at the age of three and a half years, and again it was challenging for him for many years to follow. Tying his shoes was a struggle, and fasteners were just as tricky. His speech was delayed; he spoke words at the age of two and spoke in sentences at the age of three. Potty- training was just as challenging at the age of four. He began to wear glasses at the age of three, far-sighted in one eye and near-sighted in the other. I know this is a fact: our kids love consistency and routines make their life just that much easier to navigate, especially if it's something expected of them. No surprises!

I was working full-time and was exhausted. I tried M&M treats and unfortunately I used Toys R Us trips far too many times. Back then we were all trying to figure this out. I was very consistent with teaching him everyday skills. For example, our workday mornings started at 6 am with restroom tasks, dressing self, breakfast, then off to grandmas or pre-school. All the tasks were done with me leading and talking him through each step. I did this for many years.

Martin is very inquisitive, affectionate, and tenacious, especially with his interests. He is bright and loves to learn. Waiting his turn and getting along with his peers was a challenge. He preferred to sit alone and read his books. We would read every night together, and by the age of three, he had mastered reading books by himself. I marveled at this because he couldn't hold a conversation with me, but he could read a book. Martin started to speak at the age of four, and he hasn't stopped, hence *Chatter Box.*

Martin and his love of books were apparent over the years. In his younger days, he would carry as many books as he could hold at one time. I'm laughing as I write this, but he still, to this day, carries as much as he can that's of importance to him. His wallet is bulging to the seams with all his receipt purchases and cards he collects.

Martin was always in the tenth percentile as far as height and weight. His head circumference was larger than normal. I tended to wonder what type of life he would grow to have. I pray for him daily, knowing God's got this. When he was a baby, he would wake up every one to two hours for feedings or just being fussy. I remember so many nights, not sleeping at all and running off to work exhausted. On a side note: our aspie kids don't mean to call names or scream. They can't verbalize or understand, and so they become impulsive and say what's on their minds, good or bad. To a degree, it's refreshing to have so much honesty.

Martin had spine surgery because of a hemangioma tumor on his spine, and he also had scoliosis. Martin is a huge sports fan, and so the night before his surgery, his father and I threw a party for him at the local baseball game. He grinned from ear to ear, called the game, and ran the bases. They performed a 14-hour surgery to reconstruct his spine. He now lives with two rods and eighteen bolts holding his upper body together. He was a trooper during recovery. I'm so proud of him! When I brought him home from the hospital, I set up a twin bed in my room so I could care for him. He had some tough nights, and would wake up crying so loudly from the pain. I would calm him down and pray to God to help Martin and me through this. He did!

About four months after Martin's spine surgery the strangest thing happened to me. I had an aneurysm brain bleed. It's kind of helped me to understand Asperger's a little more. For some time, everything seemed foreign to me as well. I remember thinking one evening, "Is this what Martin goes through?" I had this overwhelming feeling of compassion for him. I learned to be more patient. I needed help from everyone around me. I had poor balance, loud noises hurt, forget my topic of conversation at times. I struggled to read books, my words were scrambled and I was sensitive to touch. I wanted to scream some days; I didn't understand who I was.

Martin tends to get down on himself and gets frustrated with what he can't figure out. If there is something I could say over and over to Martin, it would be that "we are perfect the way we are". God doesn't make mistakes. Martin has taught me to accept, to laugh with his quirky jokes, to understand differences, to love, and to be kind. Our guys may not understand social cues, but they do know if you like them or not. Martin has always been sensitive to older people, and I love this about him. He listens intently to their stories and plays card games with them. He would call his grandmother every day to check on her. When he was younger, he related better to older and younger folks, and less so to kids his own age. Kids his age didn't "get" or understand him. This changed when he got older, and he became more comfortable and confident with his age group.

He has a deep love for all animals. Martin spoils our dog, Hunter, every day with hugs and kisses. He has trained Hunter to do unusual things, for example, shake his head if he needs to go outside. You can hear the tags on his collar as he shakes. Also, one lick means yes. If Hunter wants a treat, he taps Martin's foot.

I've read stats somewhere that aspies have a high suicide rate. We need to learn more about supporting and understanding them, primarily through their teenage years, when they are the most vulnerable. Martin and I talk about everything. His father and I decided we would go at this without medication. **Please keep in mind this was our decision.** I thought that maybe we wouldn't be numbing his reality. I love who he is; I didn't want to alter him. I'll be honest, it was hard, and there were days when I wished we had chosen meds. We tried an anti-depressant at one point per the doctor's recommendation, and it didn't work well for him. He didn't like it, and it made him more anxious. Martin has many interests, and I think this has been his saving grace. Physical activities are essential in his life. It helps to relieve stress, and the energy build-up he has stored away. At the age of twenty-nine, Martin has decided to take anxiety meds when he finds it necessary in certain situations. He has full control of when to take them and usually uses them before a test. I have suggested, when we are attending a party and know there will be lots of people and noise, perhaps he should medicate. I've questioned my decisions quite often with Martin and still wonder to this day. It's always a learning process. We want to do it correctly, right?

CHAPTER 2

Martin: Disabilities

Now it's time to get to the real stuff like the disabilities that I deal with daily. I have a few disabilities, and they affect me in many ways. It's an uncomfortable topic, but something I need to share.

One thing I am trying to control is my inward thinking self. I tend to talk about myself a lot and talk about what I like (sports, music, theatre arts, etc.), instead of asking others about their interests and getting to know more about them. But I have been getting better, and I've been mindful, asking others how their day or week is going. If you met me for the first time, I would talk about myself instead of asking about the person I am having a conversation with. When someone comes up to me, and asks how I am, I tell them how I am doing, and then talk about one of the subjects I choose rather than ask how that person is doing. Still, I have been practicing and getting slightly better at talking less about myself. I also tend to speak loudly even though I try my best to talk softly, which I can accomplish most of the time, but not all the time. Trust me; it is challenging to keep it in check.

One thing that is challenging for me is writing. Whenever I write, I make errors like random capitalizations, run-on sentences, and comma splices.

I get annoyed by the fact that I frequently say "wait." I don't know why, and I tend to be apologetic, which can be irritating. For example, I tend to apologize when something doesn't go right even though it is not my fault; I tend to blame myself.

A symptom of Asperger syndrome is interrupting people. It is one of those big ones for me because it has been an issue ever since I started to talk. I am bothered by the fact that I have this problem. I don't mean to interrupt people, but most of the time I can't control it.

The two primary disabilities I was diagnosed with are NLD (Non-Verbal Learning Disorder) and Aspergers. I will give you some details as to how they affect me.

First, I would like to talk about Asperger Syndrome. Now, this disability is on the autism spectrum, so basically, Asperger Syndrome is a milder form of the disability. It mostly affects socializing and communicating like reading body language. Aspies have a tough time reading body language and can't tell what your feelings are - if you are annoyed, or happy, or sad, or angry. Learning how to read someone's body language or make eye contact has not been easy. Growing up with it has been super challenging, especially trying to stay encouraged. I usually get down on myself when I get discouraged. When I tried to make a friend at school, it wouldn't work. I would tell myself to just give up for the semester. I especially get discouraged when I don't pass tests; that is when the discouragement hits the most. I am socially awkward most of the time, but I try to keep it hidden because I don't want to be the one person that doesn't know how to be social. Asperger Syndrome affects me when I am at school. You can tell because I am usually quiet and rarely talk to anyone, even classmates. However, I also feel like my fear of being told "no" plays a factor most of the time. I stop myself sometimes and tell myself I should accept it because, unfortunately, I can't change people's minds.

Another symptom is aggression. Although I don't show this sign often, you will know when I am being aggressive. It is not a pretty sight. So, if someone agitates me, my aggression usually takes over. I will get in their face (even though I don't mean to), and sometimes I feel like punching a hole in the wall like I did in my room one time. During my freshman year in high school, a kid who was a senior or junior, kept picking on me. So one day before Christmas break, I hit him. I felt awful and I apologized to him, but I was suspended because I fought back. I had had enough, and when that aggression took over, I swung at him. Some of the students called me "One-Punch" Martin, and as hard as I tried to keep my aggression under control, I failed. That was the only time I ever hit someone, and I learned from my mistake.

I've also gone through and faced a lot of depression. It gets hard to shake. Depression is one of those things that has been with me for most of my life. Still, I don't show it, so what I am trying to say is, I mask it. I don't want people to worry about me. One situation that triggered depression happened after I got a bad test score. My English teacher said that I should drop the class because I wasn't doing so well. Of course, being headstrong I didn't listen. I couldn't stand the thought of being a failure. I had believed I was going to do well in that class and boy, that turned out to hurt a lot. I was masking my depression, although it was hard to keep it hidden. Depression is a hard issue to deal with for sure, and studies show that it's a lifelong ordeal for people with autism. I am usually depressed when I can't make a single friend at school (which has been the norm in college because of my fear of being told no). It hits the hardest when Valentine's Day comes around since I have been single my whole life. I usually stay in my room, blasting music, and would rather stay home instead of going to school.

I became depressed when I went into my favorite coffee shop to get coffee and study (which was almost every day). There was only one table available, but a lady was sitting there reading a paper. I approached to ask if I could sit there, but she turned her head and looked the other way. I wasn't sure if I should sit there or not and didn't understand her body language. I eventually sat somewhere else.

Most Asperger's kids like me on the spectrum tend to isolate themselves because we are afraid of large crowds, but I mostly control that fear now. I love going to sporting events and concerts on my own. One time, one of my teachers wanted me to go to one of the high school dances. I agreed to go, but that was not easy. There were so many people there, and my anxiety hit me like a ton of bricks. So most of the time I was in a corner trying not to engage in any conversation. Since I was by myself, I went out of the building trying to get fresh air because my anxiety was so high. I didn't have fun even though I tried my best to enjoy my time there.

It gets annoying when I hear people talk about me, especially during the lab parts of class. They think I don't listen to them. It's not fun when I report it to the teacher, and they get away with it.

Now on to NVLD (Non-Verbal Learning Disorder). Non-Verbal Learning Disorder is a neurological disorder that affects the way we communicate non-verbally, that is through body language, facial expression, and eye contact. I display NVLD symptoms a lot, especially tone of voice. I have a hard time speaking softly when required, like at a library. Eye contact is another challenge. Most of the time, when I'm talking to someone, I usually look around and make eye contact with them on occasion. I am working on it. I have noticed some improvement when making eye contact, but it is difficult. One of my biggest challenges is hearing people's tone of voice and reading their body language, which could be a reason why I have difficulty making more friends.

I've also dealt with low self-esteem; this symptom, I feel, is connected to depression. I have super low self-esteem when it comes to trying to make friends. It's so low that I don't ask coworkers to hang out or see if they want to get together after work because of it. I don't even think I have reached rock bottom yet, and it is super challenging to bring my confidence back up. My self-esteem has been bad lately to the point where I just want to stay in my room and not do anything. It sucks and it is very hard to cope with. I don't even think I have hit rock bottom yet.

Sometimes, out of nowhere, I get feelings of sadness, which is tied to my depression. I think the hardest part of dealing with this is talking to others. At the church I go to, I've gone to their meetups. I was reticent and rarely talked. After all, I felt like I didn't fit in, and sometimes it would get to the point where I snuck out and left, without saying goodbye. I don't talk to them a whole lot anymore because I get nervous. I feel bad for doing that. I feel like I need to bring up stereotyping since it happens to us a lot.

The news reports are frustrating because some of them portray Autism as a disease. First, it is not a disease; it is a neurological disorder most possibly caused by the prefrontal cortex being developed differently than that of a "normal" brain. One news report was about an autistic student being dragged out of the classroom by a teacher, which is not right. What do these teachers think they are accomplishing by doing something so horrible? It needs to stop. It hurts me to see when people like us get targeted, and I have this burden because I can't do anything other than tell my story. We are human beings, just different. Our differences don't make us less deserving of compassion. Teachers need to understand that and not treat us as if we don't belong in the classroom. This needs to stop.

Apparently, autistics have a higher suicide rate than other people, and it's about ten times higher than that of ordinary people. I had those thoughts mostly in middle school and high school. Depression is a significant factor with autistic people committing suicide. About seventy-seven percent of autistic kids contemplate or attempt it.

Another thing I would like to mention is if you approach us and we walk the other direction that means we don't want to talk to anyone. I did that a few times before but got some snide looks and comments from people. Some people on the spectrum don't like loud places like a coffee shop, so it's important to have a quiet and peaceful place to hang out. In contrast, some are fine with it, but it does depend on the person and if they are having a good day or not. It may take a while for them to be approachable, so be prepared to have a tough time.

One last thing I would point out, although some of us are approachable, we could change our minds and not want to be approached. I did this a few times when I decided not to hang with someone because I didn't feel safe. I think the hardest part about living with autism is that people take advantage of us, make fun of us, physically attack us, and think autism is a disease. Some people believe we are defenseless and will take the hits. Parents, I know it can be difficult raising someone like us, but you can't give up, even if it looks like there is no hope. Trust me, my mom puts up with me a lot. Sometimes we can't control our anger and sometimes we get angry in order to release our anxiety because we don't know any other way. We all need to stay strong and know we can do it. I would like for ordinary people, like kids in school that bully us, to learn more about autistic kids. Every time I've told a bully I am autistic, they seem to use me, tease me, and pick on me because they think I am an easy target. It bugs me a lot. Sometimes I tend to hurt people's feelings, like family members (though not in a while) and close friends. I don't mean to, but I'll lose my temper and hurt them and turn my back on them because I tend to feel like they aren't there for me. I am much better now at not turning my back on my family because I love them. As I've gotten older, I know that I can trust them. I sometimes get to the point where I just want to give up and let bullies continue to use me and tease me. So, all I ask of people is to learn about autism and not pick on us or use us as an easy target. I know what it is like to get picked on and not having your friends help you. But let me tell you, we are intelligent kids. We are smart and we have highly creative minds. I sometimes get picked on by normal kids to the point that I just cry. Of course not in front of people, so I don't look weak. It angers me to the point where I want to make them feel the pain like I do so they know what it's like to get bullied. Just for once, I would like people to step into the shoes of an autistic individual for a few minutes to know what it is like to have autism. Think of what you can do to help us so we can feel like ordinary people. There is no cure for autism, but with your kindness and help we can have a better life and be happier.

I want to bring up masking since I mask almost daily. I will also bring up ways to cope with it. What is masking? Masking is when someone on the spectrum mimics others to fit in with society and be unnoticed in the world.

What does masking look like? It is hard to describe, but will do the best I can to tell you. Basically it looks like we are quiet at first and this is due to us holding back as we observe the surroundings and situations. What most of us do is be like a chameleon and not express our emotions, thus leading to others thinking we are normal. One other thing is both males and females mask due to being aware of the social indifference. The reason why it is hard to tell masking is happening is because of our subconsciousness taking control. It could lead to loneliness, mental tiredness, confusion, and burnout (I experienced all of these).I created a video on masking and I was really out of my comfort zone with this one, but I did it for work and for those who don't understand what masking is. I know that it can be hard to go through but just know that you got this!

Mom: Disabilities

The meaning of Spectrum: *a wide range*

Autism is known as a spectrum disorder because it has *a wide range* of effects on our kids, and it is different for each. I think Martin sometimes appears a little odd to people. I see how they look at him, and I must admit my heart hurts when I see this. He has some social struggles. Earlier in his life, it was challenging for Martin to make friends, but now he is quite the social butterfly. Knowing his space, understanding humor or sarcasm - forget it - it doesn't work; he doesn't get it.

I believe Martin attending Social Thinking classes offered by Michelle Garcia Winner was pivotal in helping him understand friendships and relationships along with me explaining social cues daily. I would encourage him to invite friends from school, and honestly, I think feeling more confident in himself made him more confident in his personal friendships.

There was an incident where his boss attended a football game with him and had to leave early. He told Martin he needed to put out a fire. Martin thought this literally. When he came home after the game he said, "Mom, I feel so bad for my boss. His house caught fire and he had to leave the game early." I knew it wasn't what his boss meant and explained to Martin people refer to putting out the fires in different contexts. For example, maybe something happened at work that needed his attention right away.

Handwriting has always been a struggle for Martin; he has made adjustments and is a fast typist now. Sentence punctuation is tough as well. He writes the way he talks, fast and continuous.

Knowing his body space has been a challenge. I have to remind him what the appropriate space when speaking to someone is, upwards of two feet.

Finding the right medication has been a process. We tried Martin on Ritalin in the second grade per his teacher and doctor's recommendation. He didn't fare well. His tremors were exaggerated, and he looked so sad. Later in middle school we tried anti-depressants per doctor's recommendation, but Martin did not like how it made him feel so we stopped. In college, Martin talked about his anxiety and the doctor recommended anti-anxiety meds that would be taken as needed. This worked for Martin, especially before test taking; he has very high anxiety with test taking. He would take one pill thirty minutes before test and it took the edge away.

CHAPTER 3

Martin: Anxiety

Anxiety is, by far, the toughest challenge I deal with daily. The signs include a lack of interest in activities, low energy, and bad sleeping patterns as well as rapid breathing (tachypnea). Anxiety has affected me for as long as I can remember, and it's at its peak when school exams come up. Because I'm afraid of failing, I'm usually super anxious, anywhere from a week to a day before exams. I sort of connect the dots between anxiety, low self-esteem and depression. Essentially, anxiety leads to low self-esteem, and leads to depression. Anxiety sure is difficult to deal with every day. It's tough for me to talk and write about it because when I do I get this sinking feeling in my stomach. Even though anxiety takes a hold of me sometimes, I try not to let it completely affect me because I don't want it to entirely control my life. There are a couple of types of anxieties that I deal with: social anxiety and general anxiety disorder (GAD). With my social anxiety I get stressed when it comes to doing things on my own. Still, I think I finally beat that up (for now). However, it tends to bite me when I least expect it. For the moment, I am doing things on my own, like going to concerts, sporting events, and theater performances. Social anxiety hits me when I want to talk to someone at a sports event because I don't think they will be interested in striking up a conversation. Other times, social anxiety takes over at school, like when I try to talk to a classmate and they give me the cold shoulder and would rather not chat. I feel like they are not interested because I am not cool enough for them, which I've been told a few times.

General anxiety disorder has been the toughest to kick. It makes me feel horrible when I least expect it, when panic attacks hit me like a ton of bricks. Sometimes, I must isolate myself in my room, so it doesn't rear its ugly form. I also tend to get anxious at airports because of my fear of something terrible happening, which sucks.

I have general anxiety when school ends and I think I have failed my classes and didn't get good grades. My stress gets super high, and I don't have the courage to look at my grades until the next semester starts. My heart rate goes up, and I tend to lose control of my breathing. I hope that when I hang out with people that I don't show this because I would be embarrassed, and I don't want others to see that side of me. Unfortunately, anxiety has a strong hold on me. I have a tough time making friends and hanging out with people that are not family. If I go places, I usually go on my own since that is all I can do at this point until I make a friend. For those of you who face anxiety, don't give up. I know it is hard, but if you let fear take you down and take hold of your life, it will not be easy to get out of it.

One thing to look for when anxiety is affecting us is a slight dyspnea which is difficulty breathing, almost thready in a way, and also tremors.

When anxiety hits, something to do is take deep controlled breaths because rapid breathing is often an indicator of anxiety. Also, listening to calming music helps. I listen to musicals like Phantom of the Opera or Hamilton, and that helps me a lot. I know it is not easy to control, but I believe everyone has what it takes to manage anxiety, although it does take time. I believe that the most significant cause of low self-esteem is social media. Social media is like a trap because, in some sense, people can easily bully others behind the comforts of their keyboard.

The "grammar police" are always active on social media. It is annoying when I misspell a word on social media because there is always that one person who obnoxiously corrects my spelling. The best thing to do is let it go because it gets ugly quickly. Trust me, I learned that the hard way when I clapped back at someone and told them to mind their own business. Although it is fun chatting with You-Tubers and athletes, it still gets obnoxious when the so-called grammar police correct my sentences. Interactions can be worse; there have been times when people would make rude comments like "drink bleach, why don't you."

I call cyber-bullying a big continuous cycle. Social media leads to cyber-bullying, which in my case leads to depression but also, in some cases, suicide. It's like a big cycle, as well as an uncontrollable wildfire (metaphorically speaking). The million-dollar question is, will this wildfire of a circle end? I hope it does because it has gotten out of hand, and no one deserves to be bullied either virtually or in person.

One last thing that I struggle with in the anxiety aspect is the Spiral of Silence. What is that you ask? It is something that happens when I really try to vent or when someone asks me what is wrong I get this "spiral" and the words cannot come out. To this day it happens when my anxiety is bad, and it is annoying because I am not able to tell someone what is wrong and I try to tell my view of a certain topic but I have the fear of being picked on and not being allowed to hang with others. A little more about this "spiral" is it was proposed by German Political Scientist Elisabeth Noelle-Neumann in 1974. The way my mind works is if I am afraid to say something then I don't speak and walk away. I have tried so hard to keep my hopes up in saying what I want to, but in the end the "spiral of silence" drags me down like a vortex. There will be times where I want to give up and have anxiety control me since I can't get out of my comfort zone, but something tells me to push forward and keep going.

Mom: Anxiety

Martin has, at different times of his life, shown signs of anxiety. It took some time to figure out what was best, and as soon as you figure it out, it changes again. When he was younger, a toddler, his way of comforting his anxiety was carrying a box a cereal. He would just nibble on Cheerios. When he began elementary school, one of his methods of calming himself was holding as many books as he could. Just his favorites would do, and he had many favorites: *Captain Underpants, Manga, Eagle Strike,* and one on whatever animal he was studying at that time. Once middle school happened, it became a little trickier. His anxiety quadrupled, and he started acting out a little more than usual.

During this part of his life, video games became more important to him. I also started a game day on Wednesdays, at his school during the lunch period. It brought together the kids on the spectrum, and some not, in a more enjoyable way. It became very popular with the students and it gave them, a time-out from whatever was troubling them. High school was intense. Luckily, he had great teachers that showed support, and in fact, he is still in contact with them.

But in high school came fundamental body changes and big mood swings. Also, keep in mind, Martin was never on any long term medications. Still, we did decide this was an excellent time to join a gym and get a personal trainer. Martin has spine issues. He needed to learn to exercise correctly. This choice helped him tremendously; it gave him excellent healthy life skills. He still works out regularly and is very aware of what his body's needs are.

CHAPTER 4

Martin: Hobbies

One of my favorite activities is snowboarding. Snowboarding is fun for me because of the rush of cold winter wind blasting on my face, and it gives me a rush of energy. I go snowboarding at places that make it easy for me to learn and ride. It's harder for me to learn at places like Kirkwood. One of the areas that I snowboard at is Heavenly because the runs are easy. When I need a break, I just head to the restaurant, eat, have a drink, relax, and do another round of snowboarding. I used to snowboard at Sierra-at-Tahoe because the runs are a bit calmer but still challenging. I have better balance while going downhill, and the food there is incredible. Bear Valley is fun too. If I do snowboard there again, I must go down the mountain slower because the runs are a bit steeper than the other resorts. I have fallen many times there, but still, I had fun despite the challenge Bear Valley threw at me. I enjoy it even though for a while my doctor didn't want me to snowboard because of my back. Now I snowboard a bit, but I must be careful. Before I turned to snowboarding, I was a skier just like my dad and my brother but made the switch because all my cousins are snowboarders. My family used to go on ski trips up to Kirkwood. We had a house in Kirkwood that we built. It was fun to live in. It was a three-story house with big rooms and lots of space. I would say the best time I had at the house was when we had Christmas together, and I had a friend sleep over.

In 2009 I went to see my doctor up in Oakland, and I found out that I was able to play soccer again since my back was fine. When I heard that, I was thrilled because I get to play the sport that I had loved since I was four. Soccer, to me, is pretty much a big part of my life. It would be sweet to coach the game because I love the game, which I mean sincerely. When the Premier League is on at 4:30 AM (West Coast California time) every Saturday morning, I am up at 4:15 AM ready to watch until 9 or 10 am when the last game ends. Also, during the last World Cup, Avaya Stadium had a watch party for all games. So, during the weekday, I would wake up at 3:30 AM to go to the 4 AM game, then go to school during the morning game, then go back to watch the 11 AM match. I did that during the Whole World Cup. It was not easy, but it shows that I love soccer.

Soccer is one of my favorite sports because the atmosphere is great in England and is now gaining popularity here in the US and Canada. I love all the energy that the fans give; it is just amazing. I also love it because I love the way the teams have their own styles of play, as well as knowing who to pass to, and utilizing the attack.

My uncle played soccer for a semi-professional sports team in San Jose, and he was good. He was a solid scorer and was very impressive. When he had the ball, he would juke the opponents and do impressive spins and then score. He kicked the ball hard, and he did what is called a bicycle kick. A bicycle kick is challenging to learn. He taught me some things like how to juke, pass, and score which I am grateful for. Another thing I do is play Football Manager, which is a PC game for people who want to know what it is like being a soccer coach. I play this game a lot. It is challenging since you have to set tactics every game, scout players, set up training, even go through media interviews. There are a few football/soccer managers that inspired me. Sir Alex Ferguson, Matias Almeyda, Jurgen Klopp, Diego Simeone, Jose Mourinho, Arsene Wenger, and Fernando Santos. If I were to meet them, I would thank them for being great coaches and for how much they inspire my aspirations of coaching the game.

I know being a coach is stressful because I went through a year of big-time struggles as a volunteer coach for a kids' basketball team. There was an assistant coach that took over a lot, which bugged me a little. If I were to coach another season, I hope I don't end up with him. I admit, though, I did struggle a little communicating with my kids. I think that is what made it an almost winless season. The only win we got was when one of the opponents in the playoffs forfeited due to a lack of players.

Playing a sport will come with enemies, and let me tell you, in the soccer class I was in at West Valley College I had an enemy. He usually delivered cheap shots that irritated me, and at one point, I almost retaliated. But I knew that if I did, I would have been dropped from my class and possibly suspended or kicked out of school.

I play with passion and energy. Whenever I'm playing a sport, I bring enthusiasm and energy to fire up my teammates and try to help lead to a victory. Sometimes I would get passionate and showboat a bit, but that may not have been a good idea. In my opinion, showboating is annoying, especially when the people showboating are ignorant. The arrogant types of players bug me a lot too, because they pretty much always rubbed it in that they scored. I did score some sweet goals during class, and the students were impressed.

I've got to shout out to the University of Iowa. Their Football team has a great tradition. After the first quarter, both teams, refs, coaches, and fans wave to the kids in the hospital next to the stadium. I tear up a bit and am thankful that Iowa recognized that there are kids that need special attention.

Gaming is fun when you are bored and have nothing to do. When I have nothing to do, I play Overwatch, PES, Madden, or other games. I would love to go to game developers' campuses like Blizzard and EA to learn how they create fantastic games. Currently, I am into Overwatch. Man, that game is fun. I love the competitive nature it brings on. I may even compete in the Overwatch league if I am ever good enough. I have been in some intense battles and love every minute of it. I also follow a couple of teams in the league (Dynasty and Shock to name two).

The downside to gaming is dealing with rude people. I had a bad game and in between rounds, the message said to all players was that they should avoid me. It did upset me. I replied, saying, "Yeah, I know I am terrible, but I will turn things around." That is one thing to be careful of if you play, and if you do run into those kinds of people, just ignore them or mute the chat, so you don't have to hear them.

I love flying and have gone with my dad, he's a private pilot. I've even gotten to control the plane, which is neat. So getting my pilot's license to fly a Baron or something would be really cool. Flying would give me a sense of freedom in a way, but of course, it would be incredible to get a ride in some fighter jets like the F-15 or F-14. I listen to an app called Live ATC, and it helps me understand what Air Traffic Control is telling pilots. I think it would be cool to go in an ATC tower and get to know what it is like directing traffic. Although, at times I feel I am Sierra Oscar Lima about pursuing my pilot license since I have been busy with school. However, as school is coming to a close, I have more time and am able to study for my license.

It can be a scary experience for kids on the spectrum when they go on their first flight. Sky is a non-profit company that helps families prepare for flying. It's uncomfortable and frightening when the plane gets bumpy. I strongly encourage parents to keep them calm during the TSA screening because it can be stressful. And even to this day, I get stressed going through it. There is so much stimulation, too many things to do, and you need to do them quickly. There isn't time to think and too many people are rushing you. When the metal detector goes off, the sound is scary. Overall, the situation is chaotic and stressful. However, once I get through the checkpoint, I instantly relax.

Another time to keep kids calm is when the turbulence hits; it can get stressful. Shout out to Autism in the Sky for doing their best to help, and they seem like a great place for people in the vicinity to go to for preparing. The next key when booking a flight is to find the right seat. For example, with me, middle and window seats are not for me because the space is small, and I tend to breathe more rapidly and get uptight. So, I always try to sit in the aisle because it is easier to get up and not interrupt others.

My family and I have done many things, but my most memorable trips were London, Paris, and Rome with my mom. My mom chaperoned me and some other kids from my high school. We went to the Vatican and went to the Louvre and saw the Mona Lisa. That painting is small and a pain to take a picture of, because it was behind a glass case and there was an annoying long line of people wanting to see it. We went to the top of the Eiffel Tower which was picturesque but super windy. We saw monks at the St. Francis of Assisi church. The best part about the trip was everything! We went to Hard Rock Café in London and took the Jack the Ripper tour. We also saw where the Beatles recorded their music and walked across the sidewalk that was on one of the Beatles covers, "Abbey Road".

Between London, Paris, and Rome, the place I enjoyed the most was probably Italy because the locals were amiable and helpful. And my mom was able to speak Portuguese so getting though Italy was a bit easier.

We also went to Mexico. We stayed in La Paz for a few days and went fishing. I remember a crab pinched my finger and it hurt a lot. I was crying and running while trying to get it off. My dad was trying to stop me from running. But I just kept running and running and running, and finally, my dad got me and got the crab off my finger. When I went fishing with my dad in La Paz, I caught a baby shark and even though we had to let it go, it was still cool to catch something.

Mexico is one of my favorite places because of the food. Their food is excellent and spicy, just the way I like it. Mexico has great weather, and the sporting events are fun. Mexico is one of those places that you might like, or you might not like. I am the kind of person that likes Mexico. It would be cool to go to a couple of soccer matches there and experience the atmosphere.

Hawaii was another fun destination, and I had a great time fishing with my dad. I reeled in a nice Dorado yellow color fin with a dark bluish body. For a 22.5 lb. fish, it put up a good fight. Next time I go to Hawaii, I would love to go parasailing which I tried it at Catalina Island and had a blast. Hawaii is one of those places where I would love to go to every chance possible because the weather there is outstanding.

I love my dad a lot even though we have been through tough times. Sometimes we don't get along but I love him unconditionally. My dad, in my opinion, is wonderful. We have done many things together. Besides going fishing in Mexico, Maui, and Santa Cruz, we have also gone to many sporting events, like the Giants, the Sharks, the 49ers, and even the As. He had a sailboat in Alameda, and we go out on the weekends that I am with him. We sail around the Bay and to Sausalito, Tiburon, and Angel Island. The boat tilts a lot, and that scares me. For some reason, I have never gotten used to it.

We've gone dirt biking in Hollister, which is fun, even though I couldn't go riding for a while. I get a rush of adrenaline from the speed of the dirt bike. I would say the most fun times I have with him are on the sailing and ski trips because I get to spend more time with him. He is a great dad.

Another fun thing we did was go to the British Virgin Islands. It was fun because we sailed all around the islands, got to snorkel, and saw a lot of cool things. We saw jelly fish and a few barracudas. I freaked out a bit because the barracuda would follow me. I was scared and underwater, I said, "Oh shoot!" Even some others heard me say it, ha-ha. However, it was still cool and exciting to see one up close and personal with its mouth opening and showing its teeth.

Now I know golf is frustrating, but it is fun to play if you have the patience for it. I golf here and there but hope to golf more when I am finished with school. I do have some golf courses in mind that I would love to play. I have taken lessons but I'm still not very good. I know it will take some practice, but I will when I have the time. I usually golf with my dad in Tahoe, which is fun, but when the wind kicks in, it's tough to play. During my twenty-seventh birthday, I spent a weekend in Cabo and played at this gorgeous golf course, The Quivira. It was tough, but I enjoyed it. I would absolutely play there again.

I know the perfect way to practice is by going to a driving range. I had some, should I say, interesting occurrences. When I swung the club, I fell a couple of times because I lost my balance. A few times instead of hitting straight, I hit towards the golfer next to me. Definitely one of my more embarrassing experiences.

I remember once when I was golfing at Eagle Ridge, a local course. The wind was rough, so hitting the ball straight was not easy. At hole four or five, I made a great 48-foot bogey putt. After that, it went downhill. I got stung in the neck by a bee; my shots went left and right; and even once I shanked it at a person's house in the back nine (I felt bad about that one). I know my golf game will improve, but it will be tough since my patience isn't that great. All I know is that *patience is a virtue*, and patience is what it will take to get better at my game. I notice when I am going down, my wrists tend to move the club head towards the ground, but I backed up before I make contact with the ball (unless it is a user error that I need to work on). I do know one thing; I have a long love-hate relationship with the driver because, at times, I can hit well with it, but the majority of the time, I just can't hit the ball straight.

Hockey is terrific, of course. My favorite position is goalie because of the intense work it takes having to try to stop the puck. Before my back problems, I started to work on being more flexible since I decided I wanted to be a goalie, knowing that it's the most stressful position. I tried to play but found that it was really hard. Still, the goalie is the one that wins games and makes spectacular saves. All in all, goaltending is one of those positions that is the most entertaining, but most stressful. Of course, it is the most important position to win the games.

I have been going to the gym for a long time, and I have to say, my current gym, Brick House, is the best ever! The staff is super helpful and nice along with the other gym members.

The next thing I like is World Wrestling Entertainment (WWE). I know it is not real, but it's still entertaining. I remember going to my first WWE event in San Jose in 2017. The sponsoring company comes up with different names for the events, and this one was named "Payback." It was awesome to see it live. The atmosphere was great, and the action was cool. It made me want to wrestle. I forgot they light fireworks before the show, and so I jumped after they announced the name of the event.

Anyway, I never tell people that I like wrestling because they tend to make fun of me. But honestly, it's just like theater with action. One of the best matches I watched on TV was John Cena vs. The Rock at WrestleMania in Miami. The crowd was so electric that it almost felt like I was there. WrestleMania is one of those unique events that put on an excellent show for millions of people worldwide every year, and it is spectacular. One day I hope to witness it in person and be with the thousands of screaming fans.

After meeting one of my favorite Manga artists, Jody Steele (who was so rad) at the 2019 Crunchyroll Expo, and after seeing her fabulous artwork, I was inspired to start drawing. Art allows you to express yourself. Art is truly remarkable in the sense that you can express yourself visually, and it gives you the freedom to draw your thoughts.

I really enjoy music. I play six different instruments: violin, saxophone, trumpet, piano, drums, and guitar. Recently I have been playing the guitar a lot because when I strike the chord it makes such a beautiful sound. Guitar playing is a part of my life. All I have to do is get out the guitar and play music; it relaxes me. I have been writing my music recently, even though I am not good at it yet. I dream of starting a band one of these days. And I am hoping to record music. If rock music doesn't work, then I can give rap a try. The beats accompanying the singers are rad. One artist I like is Lecrae. He knows how to get attention with some solid beats.

Another thing I would love to do is be a DJ. I'm inspired by Alison Wonderland, Charlotte De Witte, Dillon Francis, Diplo, Flosstradamus, Tiesto, Slushii, Zomboy, and GG Magree, just to name a few. They make me want to get into DJing. I do have a beginner DJ deck, a Numark Party Mix with built-in lights. It is the perfect way for me to practice. I hope to start at small parties and work my way up. I need to find an awesome DJ name, which is tough for sure.

I have a big passion for music, just like I have a passion for sports, and I am glad to have the wonderful gift of music. I am thankful for being musically talented and having the opportunity to play numerous instruments. Music is a part of my lifestyle; I listen to music every day.

I've thought about being a musician, but I struggle with performing in front of people. I guess it's because all the people watching me makes me nervous. I have performed in the past, but when I did, I struggled. I was breathing hard, and my heart was beating fast. It was all because I was nervous, and autism, in a way, makes it hard. I do well when I am not in front of people because no one is watching. I think I have no shot at being a career musician because my autism would make me nervous, so maybe a music major is out of the question, but I am not sure yet. Some music genres I like are Broadway musicals, Latin, metal, rap, country, and rock. I would love to learn Latin dance; it is such a beautiful and magical style. There are three styles I know of, flamenco, tango, and salsa. I think it is magical dancing to the Latin style.

I would love to travel to different places like Norway (I have some family I have not met that live there) Japan, South Korea, Portugal (to visit family), and Russia, to name a few, mostly for the nightlife and scenery for photography. I would also love to travel back to England for football matches (Premier League and Champions League because the atmosphere is amazing). Some of the top places on my list are Oslo, Norway; Seoul, South Korea; Tokyo, Japan; Moscow, Russia; Lisbon, Portugal; England; and Australia.

Finally is photography. I got a camera for a project I am working on, and so far the pics I have taken turned out great. The camera I use, the Sony Alpha 6100, is amazing. It blows my mind with the quality of the photos and video. I have taken many pics and plan on making them it into a photobook once I am finished. My main goal is to get pics of sporting events along with wildlife. I also want to get pictures of buildings in foreign countries to show the different cultures. I want to take pictures of the autism community to show a side that not a lot of people see and know to bring awareness and show that we are an amazing group of people. I am also going to be using the camera for some video recording for my YouTube channel as well. The goal for my channel and the photobook is to inspire others and show a side of the autistic community that as stated before not many people see, and to help other autistic people.

Mom: Hobbies

Martin has many hobbies. He's never still and always has something up his sleeve. He is watching, trying, or fixing sports. What I mean by fixing is, he makes up new or better plays for whatever the sports season is. He has a very visual mind, and plays come to his head. Besides sports, he also likes to work out in gyms and figure better ways to make himself healthier and stronger. Some of his other hobbies consist of gaming, golfing, soccer, and exploring everything he can.

When we travelled to Europe there were a lot of preparations to make ahead of time. We try to prepare for situations that could happen. For example, what if Martin got los,t what would he do, where would he go? I had him research the countries and customs. He even took up learning the languages. If he felt overwhelmed or tired, he would need to tell me and not wait until it was too late.

We have always encouraged Martin towards the freedom to explore! I found that our kids love to learn and to know. Join them!

CHAPTER 5

Martin: Friendships

My friend Dustin is a cool person to hang with. We have been friends for about five to six years now, and we have done a bunch of things together. We have gone to Sharks games and been to Great America amusement park. He has some pretty cool Sharks tickets, like center ice a couple of rows from the ice. I am glad to have a friend like that, and I hope we will always be friends. We've played many Halo games and Doom. We go to movies over at Oakridge Mall. We have also gone bowling at 300 Lanes across the street from Oakridge Mall (now called Bowlero), and he has beaten me a couple of times. However, I got back and beat him once. We plan on going again. I hope the next time I play him that I will beat him for the second time, unless he has gotten better without telling me. Still, it's alright, I'll figure out a way to beat him, and I'll be glad to start a winning streak of my own.

Making friends is hard because when I try to hang out with someone, I get turned down and it hurts a lot. When the school semester started back up, I just decided not to talk to anyone and be by myself, because I believed that I wouldn't have the chance to make a friend. It is almost liked an endless waltz because it repeats itself at the beginning of each semester. I feel like it's hard to make a friend as an aspie because of social awkwardness. I honestly feel like I will always have that difficulty, as much as I don't want to accept it.

I remember who bullied me as well and the horrible teacher I had in elementary school. I did not enjoy being at school because of how people treated me. I got in trouble a lot because I was tired of how the people were acting. In middle school when I got overwhelmed, I would go to the nurse's office and hide out a bit, which helped. The nurse was very supportive. On the bright side, I made some friends, although I was shy and it took a while to warm up. My favorite school experience was for my fifth grade graduation, when my mom gave me and my friends a limo ride to a park for a graduation party. I tried to communicate with my friends, but I couldn't. It was hard for me to pick a topic or start a conversation. Sometimes I would doubt that they would remember who I was. It was a real roller coaster ride before middle school. The teachers would get mad at me, kids would bully, I was suspended a couple of times, but, on the bright side, I got the principals' award for getting straight A's. There are some things that I wish I could remember to remind myself that things were better than I realized back in the day.

When I get stressed out, I do a couple of things: take deep slow breaths, listen to background rain sounds, tell anxiety it has no control over me, and listen to calming music. Now that I'm an adult, I would say I have had some good things happen. I got good grades in my Medical Assisting classes and graduated in the spring of 2019. Now that school is done, I would love to work for a sports team and help athletes become better and keep them injury-free.

I have thought of some things to help break out of my shell, and one idea is to do vlogs for YouTube or something like that (I have not started yet). I know it won't be easy with my anxiety and isolation, but in the end, it could work out. YouTube is tricky because you won't be able to please everyone. There will always be that one person who dislikes it. But I will try not to let that get to me.

Building relationships has been a challenge. For some reason, I don't get along with people my age. My relationships with specific age groups are great, like young kids and the elderly. I don't understand why I have issues with other people my age. I get along with little kids. I like to play with them, do things like basketball, card games, and even Nerf Wars. And let me tell you, Nerf Wars are fun and gives me a rush of adrenalin when I play.

I love babies because they are so cute, and I love holding them. I also take great care of babies, except when they need a diaper change; it grosses me out a lot so I almost hurl. I am never good when it comes to diaper changes, so I let somebody else do it.

I get along great with elders, and I also help them out. I have helped a few elders with their gardens, mowing their lawn, as well as assisting them with their groceries. It just pains me to see the elderly struggle with things. I love my grandma. I would call her and check in on her, and I helped her in the garden when she needed help. My mom and I take her grocery shopping. I used to bring her lunch like the Filet O Fish from McDonald's. We talked about sports, especially Portuguese soccer, the San Jose Sharks, San Francisco Giants, and even the San Francisco 49ers. I remember the days when I spent the night at her house when I was a little kid, and I had fun over there.

My grandma had major heart surgery and had to be operated on six times. I got nervous and I almost cried because of what she went through, and I thought I was going to lose her. She made it through the surgery, and after four days in rehab she was able to return home. By the grace of God, she was able to do things on her own. She didn't need help walking and could get up by herself as well.

Unfortunately, she passed away later and boy, that was the toughest loss I had to deal with to this day. It is like a piece of me will not come back. I was so close to her, but I know she is in a better place now. The day she passed, there was a verse that popped up on my phone, and I had the feeling I needed to tell her Psalms 73:26 KJV "My flesh and heart faileth: but God is the strength of my heart, and my portion is forever." I am struggling a bit still, but I know she is with me.

Befriending people my age is hard. I am disappointed that nobody wants to be my friend. I am an easy target for them to bully. I try to fight back, but I am the one that gets in trouble the most, and I just don't understand why people bully me and try to pick fights but they are not the ones that get in trouble. I think the reason why I don't get along with people my age is because they don't respect me, which is upsetting.

I have had trouble making friends since middle school, and even to this day, I have difficulty making conversation. If you were to see me at school, I usually am by myself drinking my morning coffee, studying, and listening to music. And in the classroom, I typically stick to myself rather than talk in a group because I wouldn't know how to speak or what to say. I am working on it, but it is no easy task. I feel like since I don't know how to communicate with people, it has made things super tricky.

If I go places, I usually go on my own since that is all I can do at this point until I make a friend. I get nervous talking to people because of the fear of how they will react, and there are times I hear people say stuff under their breath about me. Still, I do my best to ignore it, which gets me in a cycle of silence. Although I get out of it, it is hard to stay out of that relentless vortex. Talking to others has been a struggle for me for some time, so if someone (which would be a rarity) comes up to me, I may be super quiet at first. I am working on trying to talk to others and get to know them, especially at work, because I can't control my anxiety, which is a pain.

Mom: Friendships

He always says, "I don't have any friends."

Wrong!

I think he has made some terrific relationships along the way. He doesn't have a lot, but the ones he has are special people who like what he has to say and appreciate his knowledge and take from a different angle.

It is difficult for Martin to understand relationships. For example, he may be a little selfish or inconsiderate of the other person's feelings, not on purpose but the opposite. He doesn't understand or express emotions, so in actuality, he is very interested and is trying to navigate the relationship. With our aspies, you have to say what you mean, no gray area!

I've been witness to Martin starting good conversations with strangers. He usually chooses the topic of sports, which he is the most comfortable with, and it goes on from there.

CHAPTER 6

Martin: School & Teachers

When I started school, my parents researched a private school for kids on the spectrum called Stanbridge Academy. It was tough at first but also good. We explored a lot, much more than other schools I attended. We went river rafting, camping, and had beach picnics. I went there for two years. Finally, the long, long drive down Mt. Hamilton to San Mateo proved to be too much and I started attending public schools.

Problems escalated when middle school came around. I remember I was in band class and missed a beat, and because of that, my teacher got into this angry rage and yelled at me. Another teacher that agitated me was my art teacher. Once I forgot to bring a pencil to class, and I got sent to detention which didn't make sense. He didn't like me, that's for sure!

My second year was terrible, for I was always getting bullied. I fought back multiple times. One bully kept on demanding I give him money, or I would get beat up. I did the first couple of times but stopped and tried to avoid him, and after letting school administrators know, he got a suspension. I thought it was over, but oh no, it continued. There was another bully I fought back against, but that time I got the suspension. The bully didn't since I attacked out of frustration. The hardest part about coming back from my suspension was finding out that the bully was now in the same class as me. So, I was nervous and skipped class a couple of times. When I talked to my family about the bullies, they were sticking up for me and were there for me when I needed it. They spoke with administrators and teachers to make sure that I was to be in a safe environment. So, my mom set up a lunchtime meet up in one of my teacher's classrooms for all the students who were bullied and had disabilities. We hung out, ate lunch, and played games in a safe environment.

Despite the negative experiences, I've had some very good teachers that I loved being taught by. The first teacher I liked was Mrs. J. She was such a great teacher; she helped me with my spelling because I was a *really* bad speller. After spelling tests, if the class got a good grade, she would show us a movie and give us treats. She was really kind and understanding. In middle school, I had two excellent teachers. One of them helped out a lot when I was dealing with bullies. When I struggled with homework, she helped me fix mistakes I made on the assignments. She is, and was, a great teacher. In high school, I had three excellent teachers. The first one was my government and science teacher; he taught both. He was a great teacher, and it was fun learning what he taught us. Every time I was in class, he did some cool activities, like play games, and if it was an early morning class, he gave us coffee. He was a laid-back teacher. The other excellent teacher I had was my high school math teacher. I've always disliked math. She made learning math fun with activities and such and some days she would play movies. We did some projects like building things with toothpicks. I think I made a sports stadium. She was just a great teacher that helped me when I struggled in class, which was a lot.

Finally, my favorite teacher was my teacher for seven years from grades 6-12. She helped me when I was dealing with bullies. We still communicate here and there. Sometimes we run into each other at a grocery store and once or twice, at a coffee shop. She helped me study for the High School Exit Exam, which was the most stressful test I have ever taken. It took four years to pass. Can you believe it, four years? I bet I was the only student in high school to fail the exit exam three years straight. I never went through so much stress as I did with the exit exam. I probably snapped at least thirty pencils because I was so frustrated. I finally passed my exit exam when I was a senior. I found out that I passed on a chilly night on Cinco De Mayo. I was so happy; it felt like a huge weight was lifted off my shoulders. I give God the glory for it. That test sure challenged my mentality and stress levels throughout high school. I did almost give up at one point because I felt like I would never be able to pass it and graduate high school.

When it was time to go to college, I thought of majoring in game design, but the hard part, is that creating the 3D world involves math, which I am not good at. Another major I thought would be perfect was sports medicine because I love sports. I like to play them, and I wanted to be in the medical field.

My experience at school has been difficult. To be honest, being in college was a struggle. I have a hard time with tests because the tests are timed. Since they are timed, I tend to get more stressed out and blow it. Some teachers have recommended that I drop certain classes because I was struggling. I was upset and a little sad, but I did not show my emotions because if I did, I would look like a bad person. If there is one subject that is my kryptonite, it would be math. Math is my weakness. For those of you who do struggle with a specific subject, never give up because giving up on something will bring you down, and it is hard to get back up. Since I finally graduated, I don't have to be stressed out for a majority of the year.

One hard part about college is that I don't have a lot of friends, if any, so I am usually by myself most of the day. People think that I am a dumb kid and a loner, but I have tried to hang out with kids my age. It's just most of them say no, which angers me quite a bit. I have attempted to ask classmates if they want to hang out, but I get nervous and end up being quiet and walk away before they make eye contact with me. Most of the time when I am at school, I am quiet. I don't talk to others and then I head home right after. I leave directly after because I feel like I will not be able to chat with classmates or other people since I think they would not want to talk with someone like me or get a study session going.

Do I believe someday I will make a friend at school? Maybe. For those of you who want to make friends in school, never give up and be confident that things can fall into place. I believe things happen for a reason at certain times, like a blessing in disguise. So maybe, just maybe, there is a blessing involved in not making a friend in college, and maybe that friend will come when I get a job, who knows, only time will tell.

I've been the brunt of bully-attacks since preschool. When we see someone being bullied, the best option is to stop it as fast as possible. I've learned the hard way that when you get bullied and throw the first punch, you will be the one punished more severely.

When I was bullied, I was ignorant. I made the wrong decision by not telling the teachers, administrators, or my mom, and I regretted that because the bullying continued. It ended up at the point where I had to give him money every day so that he wouldn't bully me and threatened me if I didn't. To be honest I finally told the administrator, and the bully was expelled. Thankfully, I didn't have to deal with him anymore.

I had another bullying experience during PE my freshman year. I felt like I had to hit him for what he had said to me, which I don't recommend. The upsetting part about the situation was that I was suspended for thirteen days, and he was only suspended for two. I was pissed off with the administration for giving him a lighter sentence. When I got back to school, some people gave me a high five left and right, including my teachers and his friends. I was surprised.

Bullying is not cool, and it needs to stop. I feel like people who bully most likely have had a terrible childhood. They take it out on us aspies along with other people that have disabilities. I get worked up when something like that happens, and I am disappointed I can't do anything about it, as much I want to step in.

I feel like I would let my temper get the best of me. When we're being bullied, it's important to seek help.

Mom: School & Teachers

I started each year with a note and handbook - a handbook I had written myself because, at the time, there wasn't much to go on for the teacher on Asperger's kids. The handbook started with a definition of autism. Then it included personal information about his struggles, what he needed, and what he was good at. I provided family contact information, and reports from the Children's Health Council. I put together what I could from talking to doctors and other teachers with similar experiences. It would explain what Martin was diagnosed with and how to manage his situation better. Some teachers appreciated it, and others (very few – like one) did not.

I had to pick Martin up from school one day for being suspended. He had apparently threatened a kid at school. We had just placed him back in public school because the drive to San Mateo was tough. We couldn't find any other private school that could fit his needs closer to home. Martin told me the kid had been making fun of him and picking on him continuously. His teacher didn't understand him, nor did she want to. She wouldn't even take my handbook. It was a high stress classroom because she was unwilling to know him and made the situation in the classroom unbearable. Luckily, another teacher, Mrs. J, heard about the situation and asked if she could have Martin in her classroom. He soared and had terrific results in the new classroom from a teacher willing to understand. That year the principal visited each class and announced they were each going to write a book for the young author's book fair – they picked the best book from each school. Martin won the Young Book Authors Award the same year for writing *The Silverbird*.

In the early 90s I didn't have a lot of resources for Martin, so this is all we could come up with. He had Individual Education Plans (IEP) in school and was offered speech therapy and occupational therapy from elementary through high school. In college he was included in the support and services program.

I became a volunteer mom and did whatever I could to make the teacher's life easier. Martin's middle school days were tough. I noticed he would always bring his lunch home uneaten or just a few bites here and there. I asked him why, and he said, "I have no friends." At this time, we had moved, he was in a new school with new kids, and he had to make friends all over again. I decided to start a lunchroom once a week on Wednesday. I figured middle of the week to break it up a bit. It started with just the special-ed kids, and I brought board games and snacks. The kids loved it! They started to gain relationships and have lunch buddies during the days I wasn't there. It became so popular, and it wasn't just our special kids; it was kids in the mainstream that wanted to participate. Some of them didn't have any friends, or they just needed a break. They all had a terrific time. This turned out to be a fantastic way for the mainstream kids to get to know our kids, and it worked out beautifully. Towards the end of the school year, we would play water balloons and badminton. Years later, I reached out to the teacher who so kindly donated her room, and she has continued with the tradition. I was delighted to hear this.

Martin still has excellent relationships with his teachers. They keep in contact through social media or run-ins at Starbucks, Martin's favorite hangout. I sure appreciate the teachers along the way, their patience, and kindness. It made my life a little less stressed, and my insides a little calmer.

Thank you.

When it came time for college, I was nervous for him. I was scared, excited, and my stomach: a mess. We had spent the summer figuring out his schedule, getting a full load, and I honestly thought, *"you got this."*

That is not what happened. He was overwhelmed, exhausted, and frustrated. His load was too big. We should have kept it simple for at least the first semester until he got his bearings straight. He failed all his classes, but one. Martin, at this point, needed help with organization. Some advice: start with organization early in their life. There was a lot of lecturing in classes and note taking. It was hard for him to keep up, so we switched colleges and found another that was more supportive, and it was a perfect fit. It had better support programs for him. He moved right along and graduated. His counselors kept better track and developed a relationship with him. He is still friends with his counselor. He filled in for her a few times and taught her fitness class. I love that he develops relationships with people and keeps them. He began to succeed and become more confident. Once he got his confidence, he began to do his research and homework without a lot of help. He also took a private cooking class and enjoyed cooking for his family.

CHAPTER 7

Martin: Spirituality

Religion plays a big role in my life. I follow the Christian faith. God is good. When I am struggling with life, as usual, almost daily, God is always there for me. He was there during the time I had surgery. His hands were on everything in the operating room. Before I had my surgery, my mom and I said a prayer asking that everything go well and asking God to keep his hand on the doctors. Sure enough, it went well, and during the surgery, my mom and a couple of other members from the church were in a circle and praying for me, which was cool of them to do. When they were praying, a stranger walked up to them, and asked if he could join them. I thought that was nice of the man to join them. I am thankful that I am well and that there isn't much pain.

I remember when I took my driving test to get my driver's license on February 13, 2010. It started pouring down rain, and I was thinking, "Okay seriously, is this happening right now?" I think God was testing me to see how I would do in the rain. I was freaking out a lot, but passed and got a 98%, and I thanked God for that because he deserved all the glory for helping me pass the test in the rain.

I am also thankful for the time God helped me pass the high school exit exam after seven tries of studying hard and staying up late. I passed, which matters a lot because I got my diploma instead of just a certificate of completion. If I didn't pass, that would have hurt me a lot, and I would have felt miserable on grad day at the Rose Garden in San Jose.

I attend a church in San Jose, and it is a fun church to attend. It gets wild on Sundays. During the Second Service a.k.a. Jubilee Service, it gets so wild that God has spoken through people before. We have different preachers come from different churches to preach. One night, I was at the altar praying, and the preacher came up and spoke to me. He said that God was going to embrace me and lead me in the right direction. When I heard that I was surprised at first but realized that what he said to me was a blessing, and I never forgot it.

To be honest with you, I am not a perfect Christian. I don't watch what comes out of my mouth most of the time. I regret it sometimes. I say this because I get into arguments with family members, and I can get into heated discussions with other people. I don't read the Bible a whole lot. I think it's because I am, for some reason, afraid to read the book of Revelations.

Mom: Spirituality

I start my day meditating and spending quiet time in prayer, preparing myself for the day ahead. This habit has taught me to trust and have faith in Jesus.

I love how Martin loves God; he has his own prayer life and relationship with the Lord. Our aspie kids tend to be more visual, which can be difficult when you can't see something or someone. Somehow, Martin has found the desire in his heart to see and know God for himself.

CHAPTER 8

Martin: Uber

I would like to start driving more so my mom doesn't have to drive me around. she takes me to school, the mall, and the grocery store. For some reason when I drive, I get really nervous, always thinking that I will get into an accident. I need to get that fear out of me and drive my car more. I have been practicing, but the tailgaters and aggressive drivers make it hard to be confident in my driving. I know being able to drive with more confidence will enable me to get out of the house more and be independent.

I got insured so I can drive again, which is a good start. Now all I just need to do is get behind the wheel. I will be a bit nervous because I don't want to get into a car accident. But I must fight my fears because I want to start driving.

Another reason why it will be tough is because of those aggressive drivers who try to make you go faster than the speed limit, then honk at you while they speed by. A few times they gave me the one-finger salute, but the best thing to do is let it go and not start anything.

Uber has been super helpful. It can be a hit or miss, yet it is also super beneficial. It's good to use when I go to a concert or sporting event. Uber is beneficial because I don't have to worry about parking. And getting out of the area is the worst after events. Oh, and paying for parking can put a significant dent in the wallet. If I want to spend the day at the mall or go far like Monterey, or Oakland, or San Francisco, the drivers are okay with driving me there despite the traffic, and they get me there safely.

Sometimes drivers have been rude and unwilling to take me to my destination. A couple of times, I had a driver arrive at the pickup location and tell me that they wouldn't take me to my destination without an explanation. Other times I get messages saying they are too far away to provide me with a short ride. Some drivers are rude, although I understand, because sometimes passengers are rude, or they must deal with traffic. One thing that does annoy me is when you need to go to different destinations. The drivers would want you to end the ride to the first destination, then request a ride again; they say it helps them. It makes more sense to have it be one trip instead of two or more. One last thing is some drivers tend to speed, which makes me uncomfortable, but I don't say anything so they don't get mad and give me a bad rating. However, I have had many great experiences and even connected with some of them.

Mom: Uber

Uber has probably had the most profound effect on Martin, and his path to moving forward with autism. Uber has been fantastic in a way that has given him a sense of freedom and independence like no other.

When Martin got his driver's license, and passed his driver's test, he was so excited and exhausted he couldn't drive home. He was on top of the world, but it has been difficult for him. Most people, when they drive down the street, see all the important things like stop signs, people, and oncoming cars. When Martin drives, he takes in everything: signs, lights, cars, guy watering lawn, squirrel in the tree, and it becomes, at times, overwhelming to navigate safely.

Martin did not like taking the train, bus, or any other type of transportation that forced him into situations with people he didn't already know or feel comfortable with. His lack of sense of direction didn't help the situation.

On his first Uber ride it was difficult for him to wrap his head around and he didn't want to do it. If he wanted to have dinner with his father that evening, he would have to join him by taking Uber. Martin was clever in the way he handled it. He invited his cousin Jared along for dinner, and they took Uber together. Upon returning home, they both had full tummies and Martin felt a little more comfortable with the thought of Uber, but not completely convinced.

When he started taking Uber he would ride quietly and nervously in the back seat while the stranger drove him to his destinations. Before long Uber gave him the confidence and a sense of trust in people he had never had. He would start conversing, talking sports or just sharing conversation. He became more outgoing and not afraid to venture out into this new exciting territory. It has allowed him to be more active in our community, along with having a fun life. He attends sports games, concerts, and even shops by himself. He does this all on his own with no pressure and has become more outgoing with everything.

CHAPTER 9

Martin: Dating

Dating is uncomfortable for me to talk about. I am not going to lie; I am new to this and am still waiting for a chance. I don't have anybody I date, which sucks. It is disappointing because it is another year of being by myself. I have tried to hang out with others. Still, they say things like "you're not good looking enough," and it hurts my feelings a lot. I ask myself; Will I ever be able to date someone? I don't get why I am never lucky. I have been so patient for the last eleven years, and some days I think to myself that I should just give up and stay single. I don't know how much longer I can wait or be patient.

I think another reason why I am not dating is that I get nervous when I talk to girls. When I talk to girls, I tend to get tongue-tied and forget what to say. I am a nice guy, but for some reason, girls just don't see that in me. I wish I could prove to someone that I am a great guy.

Do I believe in love? No, but I'm not giving up quite yet. I'm probably very close to not believing in love. I don't even dare to ask girls if they would like to hang out and get to know each other for fear of being rejected, which has hindered me quite a bit. I want to say that I have been single since I was allowed to date, which was when I was sixteen years old. Every year, I have finding a girlfriend as my New Year's resolution. I keep telling myself to just give up and that there is no hope. I have not given up, despite being turned down and rejected also known as Rejection Sensitive Dysphoria (RSD is a feeling of strong emotional pain from rejection). So now, I sometimes wonder whether or not I should be patient or just give up and deal with the fact that I will never find someone. I am actually to the point where I think love is fake, and each year that thought becomes more consistent.

One of the things that happened again that made me sad was when a girl turned me down. I don't understand why they turn me down. Maybe it's my autism that makes me nervous to ask a girl out, or perhaps it is because I am not good looking enough. It hurts because knowing that I may not be good looking enough or something like that upsets and saddens me. One friend told me that good looks don't make a good relationship, so if someone doesn't want to go out with you because you aren't good looking enough you know that is not someone you want to go out with anyway. People that base their relationships on appearance are shallow. Some of my friends ask me, "you get a girl yet, dude?" and "When are you going to get one?". my response to them is, "Dude, I get turned down a lot, and no girl has asked me out, and I My starting to believe it will never happen at this point, but I am trying not to give up."

What frustrates me is when people show how much they love each other in front of me. When I was at this Starbucks near my house, this couple got all cuddly with each other, and that bugged the hell out of me. Another time, I was going to meet up with this girl. When I arrived, she was with this guy holding hands and hugging. I would say that I feel the most down on Valentine's Day because I don't have anyone to celebrate it with. I am usually in my room, listening to music, and doing my boring homework. Since all my friends and most family members have dates, it hurts. I am not going to lie; it hurts a lot. I would like to date someone. I have been in a couple of relationships, but they didn't last, and I was really bummed. I blame myself for them not lasting even though I shouldn't.

I think it is important to take things slow because I know it is exciting that a girl/boy is paying attention to you. But if you take things too fast, it could complicate matters. It's essential to be yourself; if they can't appreciate or understand you, then just move on. For those of you that are in a relationship, I am happy for you, and I hope it goes well. For those of you who went through a breakup, stay strong and do not give up. For those of you still waiting, don't give up. I know it is hard, but the right one will show up when you least expect it.

Mom: Dating

When I think of Martin dating, it's exciting, and yet my stomach hurts with fear. So many questions, and how could he navigate this? Will they be kind to him? Appreciate him? Enjoy him? Understand him? Martin met someone at a game. She approached him, and they seemed to have a lot in common. He was excited, and as days followed, his whole world revolved around this girl. Everything became about her, and this was making me nervous. I reminded him not to forget his goals, school, work, etc. He wanted to send her a large bouquet of flowers, but we talked a little more about it and decided the smaller would be better. She wanted him to meet her parents, and honestly, my stomach just hurt for him. I was again concerned! He came home that evening from meeting them and mentioned the evening was great, and he enjoyed meeting her parents; they were very gracious. The next day, Martin was working with me at the office. As I was answering a business call, Martin looked up at me with a terrified look and said, "She's breaking up with me." The look on his face is one I will never forget. For a moment, I forgot I had answered my phone, and I quickly asked the customer if I could call her back. I was terrified, devastated, ugh! He cried a deep cry, and the only thing I could do at that moment was lean over, grab my stomach, and say to myself "Breathe, Stella, breathe". "OMG! Martin, I'm so sorry," is what finally came out of my mouth. The next twenty-four hours were tough for both of us. He was so sad and I was sick for him. I reminded him that no one on this planet escapes from pain.

I have a terrific group of family and friends. My best friend had us over for lunch; Martin wasn't ready to eat yet. She spoke kind words to him, positive words, telling him he has every right to feel the way he feels. He even let her hug him. My sister would call or text to check up on him, along with her daughters. My younger son's girlfriend took him to a Sharks game, and my niece took him to a swanky dinner. I am forever grateful for our support system.

CHAPTER 10

Martin: Work

One of the most important things is having a job. I need one to have enough money for groceries. I would be able to pay for clothes, and I would be able to buy dinner when we go out. I would be able to pay off bills and save some money for fun things like soccer games and rock concerts. A job is one of my main goals in life, but it is difficult because people misunderstand the word autism and think it's a handicap on your performance. I also get very nervous and my anxiety kicks in when I go on job interviews. My heart starts racing and I stutter. Interviews are tough, and I can't wait to get through them. I listen to calming music before interviews to help keep my mind at peace. I would love to work for a sports team and be able to treat the players to get them back to the field and even travel with them. In 2019, I graduated with a degree in medical assisting, and I want to go on to study speech pathology.

My mother encouraged me to introduce myself to the commencement speaker after my graduation. He has a fast-growing company called Center for Social Dynamics with offices in California, Hawaii, Colorado, Los Angeles, and Portland, to name a few that serve kids on the spectrum. Pete was happy to meet me and asked me to interview at his company. I went through extensive tests and training and finally got the job after multiple interviews. My job is a behavioral specialist for kids on the spectrum. Working with kids with Autism Spectrum Disorder (ASD) has been unique and challenging, but knowing that I am going to do the best I can is reassuring. One thing I love about it is being able to do fun stuff like classic connect-the-dots that incorporate both number counting and hand-eye coordination.

No two people on the spectrum are the same. From a work perspective, I could have a client who is happy go lucky and wants to talk. Then the next, I could have someone who would rather play chase (getting them back to the table to continue session after escaping) for a whole session and won't be able to get to the planned curriculum. It has taken somewhat of a toll on me physically since I get exhausted at the end of the day. One of the things I like about working with the clients is being able to interact with them easily since I know what they go through. I know I will run into roadblocks here and there and have occasional clients that don't want me as their specialist. Is this something I wanted to do? Absolutely! I know it's hard to be accepted as a child with ASD (Autism Spectrum Disorder), and I know the kids will be on the defensive most of the time. I am someone who knows how to communicate with these kids since I grew up with ASD. I know what they go through at school. I will do my best to be better and help those in need. Once I build a rapport with the kids and they get more comfortable with me, then things will be smooth sailing. I want to be able to help these kids get better and have them live their lives, happy without having to deal with anxiety and fear.

I am honored to be helping others improve their lives. A challenge I face is keeping my confidence up because not every kid will be easy to teach or develop a rapport with. I plan to do best in giving insight to the parents on raising a kid with autism. I have seen far too many times, parents wanting to give up due to various difficulties. I decided to bring my acoustic guitar to some appointments at the client's house and play for them if music is a way for them to calm down.

I love helping those affected by autism and am grateful for the opportunity my boss has given me. I look forward to what the future holds for me and the kids I will help. I want them to realize that they need to turn negativity to their advantage and use that negativity to make them stronger.

When I was in my second to last year of college, a classmate gave me a hard time and would say things about my disability to her friends. She didn't know that it made me stronger. I pushed myself to use that negativity as a tool to study harder and pass my class. As much as I wanted to clap back at her, I would have been the one in trouble, and she would have gotten away with it. If someone gives you a hard time and tells you that you are worthless, take that negativity and use it as a positive to do better.

If there was a quote that defines working with autistic kids and adults it is this: "Autism is not a sentence; it's a story". Each person with autism has their own unique story. I am just one of many unique stories. NBC Bay Area News came to our workplace and did a segment on our project. It was a unique opportunity to show what I and other adults on the spectrum do in the company.

Recently I took on a second role with the company as Event Coordinator where I am in charge of setting up events for the autism community. I am working on developing athletic partnerships with a minor league, the San Jose Giants baseball team, the San Jose Barracudas, the San Jose Sharks, and also the pro soccer team the Earthquakes.

We are the leaders and step up to help these kids, because if no one will do it, then we adults on the spectrum will. Working at CSD has been great. The staff is super chill and my boss is a great man. One thing that I love about them is that they are so supportive of each other. The vibe in the office is great, and the trainers there know what's up. When they have training sessions, they are there for you. Occasionally they check in on how everything is going during consults and see if we need support with various things like setting up a session or how to get through certain situations. Everyone that works there is great. I am glad to be a part of this wonderful company. I am looking forward to my future with them. After one year of employment with CSD, I received a promotion to executive coordinator.

Mom: Work

Martin volunteered as a basketball coach for two years, and he volunteered at our church recording the services.

Martin didn't start working until later in life. His first real job, where he was getting a paycheck, was at Guitar Center,. They were impressed with his knowledge of music and instruments. It was only for a short time, as it was seasonal, but it was a great experience. The interview process involved group interview of about twelve to fifteen people, and Martin said this was the worst experience for him. He said it made it more challenging because everyone had different answers. I would guess this would make them feel insecure since they are comparing themselves to others. He loves music and can play the piano, violin, saxophone, and guitar.

Martin got his office experience helping me at my job with simple office tasks. Organizing is not one of his strong points.

Recently, Martin and his boss were invited to attend the Night of Too Many Stars, a non-profit fundraiser for autism. However, the event was postponed due to Covid19. When I asked Martin if he was upset about not being able to attend, he told me he was more disappointed about missing an Earthquakes soccer game.

Sometimes Martin comes home from work after having a tough day, and he sums up the day as a disaster, but I can see that he is learning from the challenges he faces and that he is making progress. I also see that he is learning more about himself and becoming more self-aware.

MARTIN'S FINAL THOUGHTS

The last thing I would like to talk about is social anxiety. I believe social anxiety is the biggest challenge. Aspies tend to be super nervous when talking to others and trying to hang out with them. I have a lot of social anxiety when it comes to communicating with people. I feel stressed when I speak. I fear people will get annoyed by me talking a lot. I think my social anxiety started my freshman year in high school because I felt socially awkward. Being the target for bullies didn't make things any easier. Social anxiety is too difficult to get rid of since it hovers over us and harasses us every day. Social anxiety affects a lot of autistic people because they are afraid of being with a group of people and of being at social events. I never realized how much it had changed me until one day I was at school. I wanted to ask a couple of classmates if they would like to hang out after class. Still, I choked badly, metaphorically speaking. The worst is at the beginning of the school year in college. The teacher would tell us to get up and walk around the class to introduce ourselves to other people and exchange numbers. Still, my social anxiety made it unrealistic. So, I wasn't able to know anyone and get someone's phone number just in case I missed class. This is the biggest issue that I have been dealing with for a while. And I feel there is no end in sight. To all those who are dealing with social anxiety, don't give up. Everything will be all right. I try every day to fight it, but it has a firm grip on me, and it is tough because I want to make some friends at least. This anxiety makes it easy to give up, and that is one reason why it's challenging.

One thing that social anxiety affects the most is confidence. I hope that it doesn't affect me when I get a job, especially if it's in a hospital, doctor's office, or with a sports team. I finished my externship at a medical facility. It was great helping as much as I could. I learned life lessons: calling people to remind them of their appointments (which was hard at first because I am nervous calling people), doing laundry, cleaning the towels for physical therapy, and cleaning gowns for the medical office. I did not like it at first because folding clothes and I are not a good combo. I am glad I had to do that because it taught me how, and now I can fold my own clothes. It has also taught me to be more social when calling patients back for their appointments. The reason I chose to be in the medical field is not because of the money, but because I love to help people when they are struggling.

I feel like writing this book helped me in so many ways, from breaking out of my shell to knowing that this could help other people on the spectrum. However, I felt vulnerable at times and wanted to give up. Still, you can't let people stop you from doing what you want, or from living your life to the fullest. You all are stronger than you think. You just have to find the confidence and courage to step up and go all out. This quote has helped me: "You will never know your strength until you have faced your struggles". I am doing a lot better today. I got my medical assisting degree in community college, and am transferring to a four-year university to continue my pursuit of a master's degree in speech pathology, so that I can become a certified behavior specialist to help autistic kids. I currently attend SJSU to accomplish this goal of mine.

Writing this book was a whirlwind of a ride, but I feel like it is great to share my story and inspire others to step out of their shell and share knowledge with those who don't know about autism. I feel like I am an advocate for autism because I support the autism community publicly. I hope that someday people will see someone with autism as a unique piece, fitting in their own way, and that we will be viewed not by our disabilities. But by our kindness, our determination, and hard work. We are our most prominent critics, and I feel like that stops us from being satisfied with what we have accomplished.

As I bring this to a close, I just want to say that you should keep your head up and live every day like it is your best and remember to be you. Don't listen to the negativity that is around; it is just trying to break you down. Don't let it affect you.

My mom is a wonderful, kind, and caring person. She is always there for me, and I know that if I need help, I can go to her. I am thankful that she wrote *ChatterBox* with me because it will help parents as well.

Parents, even though it looks like hope is lost, it's not, just dig deep and find within you the fight to help your kids. You are your child's superhero. Even though it might not look like it, they look up to you for help. Jane Hull said, "At the end of the day, the most overwhelming key to a child's success is the positive involvement of parents" and Victor Hugo said, "Even the darkest night will end, and the sun will rise."

An anonymous person said, "An arrow can only be shot by being pulled back. When life is drawing you back with difficulties, It means it will launch you into something greater. So hold on and keep aiming!"

As I draw this to a close, I wanted to thank you for reading this book. It means a lot and I appreciate it. I hope that by reading the story of my life with autism you get a better understanding of what it is like living with it, as well as being more accepting of us. Thank you.

MOM'S FINAL THOUGHTS

I AM SO PROUD OF MARTIN!

I love who he is and the adult he has become. He makes me want to be a better person. His kindnesses towards people, along with the ability to *forgive and forget* are something to be admired. My son has become successful in his own way. This isn't about money or a title, this is about feeling good about yourself at the end of the day, and honestly, I see how he feels and it's terrific. I know there will be other challenges, but taking them slowly and with thought, I know he will overcome them.

Martin has lots to be proud of, as do we, his parents!

RESOURCES

- Children's Health Council (408) 816-2018 - Palo Alto, CA. Early support for autism as well as Autism developmental evaluation, IQ/intelligence testing, speech and language evaluation, occupational therapy evaluations. https://www.chconline.org/
- Michelle Garcia Winner - Social Thinking Classes for individuals with Autism (408) 244-2005 – San Jose, CA. Social problem solving. https://www.socialthinking.com/
- Center for Social Dynamics (Martin's place of work) (408) 320-2590 - Santa Clara, CA. CSD's people and programs deliver personalized, professional, evidence-based behavioral and developmental services. https://csdautismservices.com/
- Stanbridge Academy K–12 School for students with mild to moderate learning differences and social communication challenges. https://www.stanbridgeacademy.org/
- NeuroClastic: information about the autism spectrum from autistic people. https://neuroclastic.com
- Next for Autism: transforms the national landscape of services for people with autism by strategically designing, launching, and supporting innovative programs. https://www.nextforautism.org

ACKNOWLEDGEMENTS

To my mom, Stella: thank you for raising me the right way. I know I was a pain to deal with on a daily basis, but I love you and thank you for taking part and writing your story of raising someone with autism.

Thank you to Steve Thatcher for writing the summary of the book. A special thank you to Abigail Pereira for editing my book at the last minute, and to Maya Bond for proofreading the final copy. Thank you to Jerry Escobar for designing the greatest cover ever.

My biggest achievement, so far, was this proclamation pictured. It was signed by the Mayor of San Jose to declare April as Autism Awareness and Acceptance Month. It took three months for the approval. A great victory for me and the autism community.

Printed in the United States
by Baker & Taylor Publisher Services